SSAT Elementary Level Grade 3

3 Practice Tests

Student's Handbook

Copyright © 2018 Student's Handbook
ISBN-13: 978-1719418348
ISBN-10: 1719418349

Table of Contents

Test 1 5
Test 2 29
Test 3 53
Answers 77

Elementary Level SSAT
Grade 3

Test 1

SECTION 1
30 Questions

Following each problem in this section, there are five suggested answers. Select the best answer from the five choices. You may use the blank space pr`ovided to solve the problem.

Sample Question:

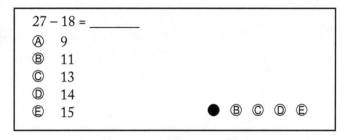

1. 377 − 129 =

   Ⓐ 248
   Ⓑ 243
   Ⓒ 241
   Ⓓ 214
   Ⓔ 208

2. On a map, 1 centimeter represents 12 miles. If I measure 4 centimeters on the map, how far is that in miles?

   Ⓐ 42 miles
   Ⓑ 44 miles
   Ⓒ 46 miles
   Ⓓ 48 miles
   Ⓔ 50 miles

3. Which is the smallest fraction?

   Ⓐ $\frac{1}{2}$

   Ⓑ $\frac{1}{3}$

   Ⓒ $\frac{1}{5}$

   Ⓓ $\frac{1}{25}$

   Ⓔ $\frac{1}{30}$

4. 54 × 42 =
   - Ⓐ 540
   - Ⓑ 2,128
   - Ⓒ 2,268
   - Ⓓ 2,568
   - Ⓔ 2,888

5. 5 − 2 + 11 − 5 + 3 =
   - Ⓐ 9
   - Ⓑ 10
   - Ⓒ 11
   - Ⓓ 12
   - Ⓔ 13

6. Sasha's birthday is in 3 weeks and 3 days. If today is July 4th, on what day is Sasha's birthday?
   - Ⓐ July 13th
   - Ⓑ July 18th
   - Ⓒ July 25th
   - Ⓓ July 27th
   - Ⓔ July 28th

7. Zephyr and Auster have 2,301 staples in their drawer. They gave 579 of their staples for 3 staplers. How many staples do Zephyr and Auster have now?
   - Ⓐ 1,204
   - Ⓑ 1,324
   - Ⓒ 1,545
   - Ⓓ 1,688
   - Ⓔ 1,722

8. If one apple weighs 3 ounces, how much do 5 apples weigh?
   - Ⓐ 8
   - Ⓑ 12
   - Ⓒ 14
   - Ⓓ 15
   - Ⓔ 18

9. $(3 + 5) + \square = 20$
   - Ⓐ 13
   - Ⓑ 12
   - Ⓒ 11
   - Ⓓ 10
   - Ⓔ 9

10. Which of the following statement is true?
    - Ⓐ 2 + 2 = 1
    - Ⓑ 2 × 2 = 1
    - Ⓒ 2 - 2 = 1
    - Ⓓ 2 ÷ 2 = 1
    - Ⓔ None of the above

11. How many quarters make up $2.50?
    - Ⓐ 25
    - Ⓑ 20
    - Ⓒ 15
    - Ⓓ 10
    - Ⓔ 5

12. ¼ − ¼ − ¼ − ¼ =
    Ⓐ 1
    Ⓑ ¾
    Ⓒ ½v
    Ⓓ ¼
    Ⓔ 0

13. What is a quarter of 5,252?
    Ⓐ 1,200
    Ⓑ 1,234
    Ⓒ 1,303
    Ⓓ 1,309
    Ⓔ 1,313

14. Which fraction goes in the blank to make a true number sentence?

    ⁴⁄₈ > _____

    Ⓐ ½
    Ⓑ ⅜
    Ⓒ ⁴⁄₈
    Ⓓ ⅝
    Ⓔ ¾

15. How many inches are there in 3 and a half feet?
    Ⓐ 30
    Ⓑ 36
    Ⓒ 40
    Ⓓ 42
    Ⓔ 46

16. 400 × 50 ÷ 25 =

Ⓐ 800
Ⓑ 1,000
Ⓒ 1,200
Ⓓ 2,00
Ⓔ 2,200

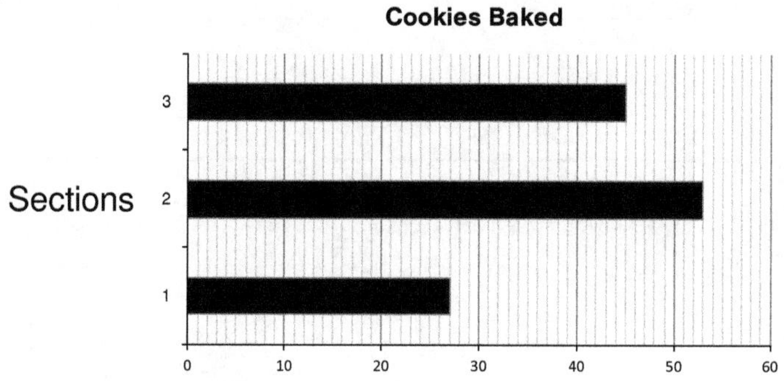

17. What is the total number of cookies baked by sections 1, 2, and 3?

Ⓐ 108
Ⓑ 118
Ⓒ 125
Ⓓ 128
Ⓔ 136

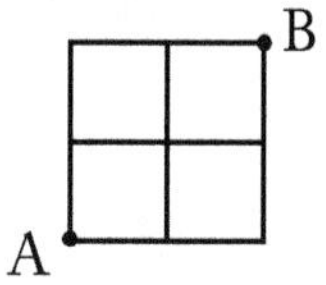

18. How many ways, going only up or right, are there from A to B?

Ⓐ 4
Ⓑ 5
Ⓒ 6
Ⓓ 7
Ⓔ 8

---

19. $\frac{2}{5} + \frac{4}{5} - \frac{2}{5}$?

Ⓐ $\frac{3}{5}$
Ⓑ $\frac{4}{5}$
Ⓒ $\frac{5}{5}$
Ⓓ $\frac{6}{5}$
Ⓔ $\frac{7}{5}$

20. How many 4-sided figures are there?
    - Ⓐ 5
    - Ⓑ 7
    - Ⓒ 8
    - Ⓓ 9
    - Ⓔ 11

21. Jenny ate ¼ of the apple pie. The entire apple cost $8.60. How much was the portion of the apple pie that Jenny did not eat?
    - Ⓐ $2.15
    - Ⓑ $4.25
    - Ⓒ $6.15
    - Ⓓ $6.25
    - Ⓔ $6.45

22. Jimmy and John weighs a total of 150 pounds. Jimmy is 20 pounds heavier than John. How much does John weigh?
    - Ⓐ 65
    - Ⓑ 70
    - Ⓒ 75
    - Ⓓ 80
    - Ⓔ 85

23. What is the area of the figure?
    - Ⓐ 25
    - Ⓑ 27
    - Ⓒ 32
    - Ⓓ 36
    - Ⓔ 40

Temperature on August 1st

Orlando	90°
Atlanta	82°
San Francisco	65°
New York	63°
Chicago	45°

24. What was the average temperature of these five cities in August 1st?

    Ⓐ 45°
    Ⓑ 65°
    Ⓒ 67°
    Ⓓ 69°
    Ⓔ 86°

---

25. What is the seventh number in the pattern: 3, 5, 8, 12, 17... ?

    Ⓐ 24
    Ⓑ 26
    Ⓒ 30
    Ⓓ 34
    Ⓔ 36

---

26. Linda wants to buy a notebook that costs $2.25. She only has $0.70. Which coins could you give Linda so that she would have exactly $2.25?

    Ⓐ 2 quarters, 10 dimes, 3 nickels
    Ⓑ 2 quarters, 9 dimes, 5 nickels
    Ⓒ 3 quarters, 7 dimes, 3 nickels
    Ⓓ 3 quarters, 5 dimes, 6 nickels
    Ⓔ 4 quarters, 3 dimes, 2 nickels

---

27. The Rogers family drove a total of 422 miles, starting on Friday and ending on Sunday. They drove 120 miles on Friday and 224 miles on Saturday. How many miles did they drive on Sunday?

    Ⓐ 72
    Ⓑ 74
    Ⓒ 76
    Ⓓ 78
    Ⓔ 80

28. There are 17 passengers waiting in line for a taxi. If at least 2 but no more than 3 passengers must go in each taxi, what is the smallest amount of taxis required to accommodate 15 passengers?

    Ⓐ 4
    Ⓑ 5
    Ⓒ 6
    Ⓓ 7
    Ⓔ 8

29. Luke scored 5, 7, 11, 13, and 4 points on five basketball games. If he wants to average 10 points per game, how many points must he score in the next game?

    Ⓐ 10
    Ⓑ 12
    Ⓒ 14
    Ⓓ 18
    Ⓔ 20

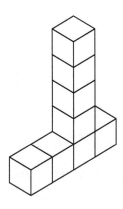

30. How many faces of the cubes does the figure above have?

    Ⓐ 29
    Ⓑ 32
    Ⓒ 33
    Ⓓ 34
    Ⓔ 36

SECTION 2
30 Questions

Synonyms
Following each problem in this section, there are five suggested answers. Select the best answer from the five choices. You may use the blank space provided to solve the problem.

Sample Question:

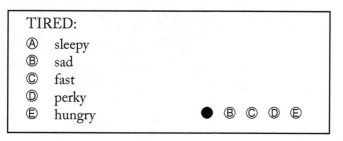

TIRED:
- Ⓐ sleepy
- Ⓑ sad
- Ⓒ fast
- Ⓓ perky
- Ⓔ hungry

● Ⓑ Ⓒ Ⓓ Ⓔ

---

1. WANDER
   - Ⓐ swerve
   - Ⓑ drift
   - Ⓒ turn
   - Ⓓ swim
   - Ⓔ run

2. VISION
   - Ⓐ walk
   - Ⓑ sight
   - Ⓒ distance
   - Ⓓ road
   - Ⓔ pad

3. SCATTER
   - Ⓐ open
   - Ⓑ dance
   - Ⓒ keep
   - Ⓓ spread
   - Ⓔ throw

4. HORIZON
   - Ⓐ blur
   - Ⓑ fog
   - Ⓒ skyline
   - Ⓓ circle
   - Ⓔ batter

5. REVISE
   - Ⓐ write
   - Ⓑ talk
   - Ⓒ think
   - Ⓓ type
   - Ⓔ edit

6. CRAVE
   - Ⓐ admire
   - Ⓑ roll
   - Ⓒ hide
   - Ⓓ have
   - Ⓔ desire

7. ANCIENT
   - Ⓐ old
   - Ⓑ fresh
   - Ⓒ new
   - Ⓓ loud
   - Ⓔ creaky

8. DELICATE
   - Ⓐ hard
   - Ⓑ big
   - Ⓒ strong
   - Ⓓ awkward
   - Ⓔ fragile

9. CLARIFY
   - Ⓐ confuse
   - Ⓑ define
   - Ⓒ arrange
   - Ⓓ lay
   - Ⓔ wish

10. CONTRAST
    - Ⓐ differ
    - Ⓑ shape
    - Ⓒ rest
    - Ⓓ burn
    - Ⓔ copy

11. ELIMINATE
    - Ⓐ glow
    - Ⓑ stand
    - Ⓒ keep
    - Ⓓ destroy
    - Ⓔ build

12. GLARE
    - Ⓐ jump
    - Ⓑ smile
    - Ⓒ sing
    - Ⓓ stare
    - Ⓔ drive

13. NUTRITIOUS
    - Ⓐ bland
    - Ⓑ nourishing
    - Ⓒ attentive
    - Ⓓ spicy
    - Ⓔ dangerous

14. NAG
    - Ⓐ agree
    - Ⓑ defy
    - Ⓒ annoy
    - Ⓓ conquer
    - Ⓔ brush

15. PARTICLE
    - Ⓐ quality
    - Ⓑ speck
    - Ⓒ oil
    - Ⓓ tone
    - Ⓔ weight

Analogies

Following each problem in this section, there are five suggested answers. Select the best answer from the five choices. You may use the blank space provided to solve the problem.

Sample Question:

> Song is to composer as
> Ⓐ book is to author
> Ⓑ clay is to sculptor
> Ⓒ hammer is to carpenter
> Ⓓ script is to actor
> Ⓔ microphone is to singer   ● Ⓑ Ⓒ Ⓓ Ⓔ

Choice Ⓐ is the best answer because a song is written by a composer, just as a book is written by an author. Of all the answer choices, Ⓐ states a relationship that is most like the relationship between song and composer.

---

16. Shoe is to foot as glove is to
    Ⓐ mitten
    Ⓑ hand
    Ⓒ leather
    Ⓓ brown
    Ⓔ arm

17. Cold is to winter as sweet is to
    Ⓐ toothache
    Ⓑ bread
    Ⓒ lemon
    Ⓓ sugar
    Ⓔ heart

18. Cat is to claw as human is to
    Ⓐ arm
    Ⓑ hand
    Ⓒ knife
    Ⓓ hair
    Ⓔ nail

19. Happy is to giggle as angry is to
    Ⓐ sing
    Ⓑ wave
    Ⓒ pause
    Ⓓ shout
    Ⓔ whisper

20. Baseball is to game as hurricane is to
    Ⓐ storm
    Ⓑ weather
    Ⓒ forecast
    Ⓓ danger
    Ⓔ rain

21. Pencil is to paper as chalk is to
    Ⓐ notebook
    Ⓑ classroom
    Ⓒ board
    Ⓓ teacher
    Ⓔ eraser

22. Day is to week as letter
    Ⓐ article
    Ⓑ word
    Ⓒ alphabet
    Ⓓ pencil
    Ⓔ television

23. Calculator is to abacus as automobile is to
    Ⓐ taxi
    Ⓑ chariot
    Ⓒ car
    Ⓓ bus
    Ⓔ trunk

24. Lion is to roar as duck is to
    Ⓐ fly
    Ⓑ quack
    Ⓒ jump
    Ⓓ flap
    Ⓔ swim

25. Apple is to pie as chocolate is to
    Ⓐ table
    Ⓑ candy
    Ⓒ coffee
    Ⓓ cake
    Ⓔ flour

26. Squirrel is to acorn as dog is to
    Ⓐ tail
    Ⓑ house
    Ⓒ bone
    Ⓓ bark
    Ⓔ house

27. Graph is to bars as novel is to
    Ⓐ chapters
    Ⓑ sheets
    Ⓒ author
    Ⓓ writing
    Ⓔ punctuations

28. tired is to exhausted as sad is to
    Ⓐ sleepy
    Ⓑ sorry
    Ⓒ excited
    Ⓓ calm
    Ⓔ sorrowful

29. car is to factory as cake
    Ⓐ pastry
    Ⓑ table
    Ⓒ dessert
    Ⓓ bakery
    Ⓔ icing

30. egg is to shell as earth is to
    Ⓐ crust
    Ⓑ country
    Ⓒ ocean
    Ⓓ land
    Ⓔ atmosphere

SECTION 3
28 QUESTIONS

Read each passage carefully and then answer the questions about it. For each question, decide on the basis of the passage which one of the choices best answers the questions.

> I love my prairies, they are mine
> From the top to horizon line,
> I love their grasses. The skies
> are Larger, and my restless eyes
> Line 5   take more of earth and air
> Than the view at the seashore
>
> I love the breeze, the never resting prairie winds
> Soothes me, brushes against my cheeks,
> I love the trees that stand like spear points high
> 10   Against the dark blue sky
>
> I love the pasture lands; the songs of birds
> Are not more thrilling to me than the herd's
> I love my prairies, they are mine
> From high sun to horizon line.
> 15   The mountains and the cold gray sea
> Are not for me, are not for me.

1. The author says the prairies "are mine" (line 1) because the author
    - Ⓐ owns the land
    - Ⓑ dreams of owning a prairie
    - Ⓒ wants to move to a prairie
    - Ⓓ feels at home in prairies
    - Ⓔ is greedy and selfish

2. The capitalization of "Larger" is to describe the skies as
    - Ⓐ scary
    - Ⓑ empty
    - Ⓒ blue
    - Ⓓ free
    - Ⓔ vast

3. As used in line 4, "restless" means
    - Ⓐ tired
    - Ⓑ young
    - Ⓒ sleepy
    - Ⓓ moving
    - Ⓔ fine

4. The trees are described as spears to describe their
    - Ⓐ color
    - Ⓑ shape
    - Ⓒ movement
    - Ⓓ danger
    - Ⓔ leaves

5. To the author, the prairie winds are
   - Ⓐ strong
   - Ⓑ comforting
   - Ⓒ ticklish
   - Ⓓ cold
   - Ⓔ annoying

6. We can infer that in the prairies, songs of birds are
   - Ⓐ melodic
   - Ⓑ everywhere
   - Ⓒ beautiful
   - Ⓓ dark
   - Ⓔ uncommon

7. The first-person speaker of the poem helps the reader understand
   - Ⓐ how the plants and animals on the prairie live
   - Ⓑ what work the speaker does while on the prairie
   - Ⓒ how other people feel about the prairie in general
   - Ⓓ what the speaker feels when looking out at the prairie
   - Ⓔ the prairie's hidden dangers

Juniper was the least important member of the house. He was loved, but no one asked him for his opinion. Everyone knew that the family's will was his will. He would follow them blindly. He was their dog.

When the family decided to move, Juniper wasn't asked for his views. The family consisted of Mr. and Mrs. Johnson and their son Buzz and daughter Charlotte.

Buzz was mad because a girl gave back a present. Charlotte had just met her handsome prince. Mrs. Johnson was annoyed that her neighbor won the art contest that she so desperately wanted to win. Mr. Adams was stressed from the long hours at work. It was safe to say that the family was in chaos.

As the family sat around the dining table, Buzz was the first to burst. "I can't go back to school. Everyone will be laughing at me."

Charlotte chimed in, "I wish I lived in a more grand house."

Mrs. Johnson sighed. "I need a place to work! No wonder I can't produce any art in this cramped place."

Mr. Johnson spoke, "Well, I need my own room after work to just relax and wind down." And then, after everyone aired their complaints, there was a deafening silence.

"That's it!" said Mr. Johnson declared excitedly. "We will move tomorrow, not get out actually, but tomorrow I'll see the real estate agent.

Having arrived at this hasty decision to move within a matter of days, the Johnsons settled down to their excellent dinner. Everyone dreamed of the new house and how it would solve all their problems. Except Juniper. He didn't know exactly what was going on but he started prancing around. Things were changing—he felt it in his bones.

8. Why was Juniper the least important member of the family?
   - Ⓐ He did not obey orders
   - Ⓑ He was the youngest
   - Ⓒ He couldn't fully express his feelings
   - Ⓓ He played no part in the family's decisions
   - Ⓔ He ate the least

9. What does it mean in line 12-13 that the "family was in chaos?"
   - Ⓐ There were in immediate danger
   - Ⓑ They were bored with their lives
   - Ⓒ Nobody was feeding Juniper
   - Ⓓ Nobody wanted to work
   - Ⓔ They were going through rough times

10. In line 14-16, Buzz is described as being
    - Ⓐ happy
    - Ⓑ tired
    - Ⓒ heartsick
    - Ⓓ frustrated
    - Ⓔ confused

11. The "deafening silence" (line 23) means that there was
    - Ⓐ an uncomfortable quiet
    - Ⓑ loud whispering
    - Ⓒ a sense of death
    - Ⓓ a loud noise
    - Ⓔ a peaceful calm

12. "Hasty" (line 27) as used in the story means
    - Ⓐ slow
    - Ⓑ logical
    - Ⓒ thought-out
    - Ⓓ quick
    - Ⓔ rich

13. In lines 28-29, the dinner was excellent because
    - Ⓐ everyone looked forward to the move
    - Ⓑ the food was finally cooked
    - Ⓒ Mr. Johnson started to eat
    - Ⓓ Mrs. Johnson prepared it with special care
    - Ⓔ the food was cool enough to eat

14. By the end of the story, Juniper becomes
    - Ⓐ happy
    - Ⓑ nervous
    - Ⓒ calm
    - Ⓓ sad
    - Ⓔ tired

One summer, I was obsessed with fresh, organic foods. I tried to persuade my parents to start eating other food. One of my goals was to introduce everyone to the wonders of brown rice.

Line 5   As a family, we were used to eating white rice. But today was going to be different. With the serving bowls in the center of the table, we filled our plates with beef, carrots and cabbage. I alone heaped a large helping of steaming hot brown rice on my place.

10   I smacked my lips aloud, trying to convince everyone to share in the new food. A half hour passed and everyone was just nibbling on the meat and vegetables. I looked down at my bowl of half-finished brown rice. I knew what was to come.

But then, my grandmother finally asked, "Did someone
15 burn the rice?"

My face turned red. My sister burst out laughing. My dad turned me to and said, "You know, your grandfather ate white rice. And he lived up to eighty years old. Sometimes, things are the way they are because they have real benefits."

15. In the beginning of the passage, the author sees brown rice as

Ⓐ healthy
Ⓑ colorful
Ⓒ disgusting
Ⓓ dangerous
Ⓔ not tasty

16. In the second paragraph, the author is best described as

Ⓐ determined
Ⓑ wild
Ⓒ crazy
Ⓓ creative
Ⓔ lazy

17. "Helping" (line 8) means

Ⓐ portion
Ⓑ gallon
Ⓒ stick
Ⓓ generosity
Ⓔ stain

18. The author "smacks" his lips (line 10) because he wants everyone to

Ⓐ talk and enjoy the food
Ⓑ be full and happy
Ⓒ eat less meat and more vegetables
Ⓓ try the brown rice
Ⓔ notice his face

19. The author "knew" what in line 13?
    A) Nobody liked him.
    B) The vegetables were overcooked.
    C) He didn't like the food.
    D) Nobody noticed that there was no white rice.
    E) His plan failed.

20. The sister burst out laughing because she
    A) did not respect the author
    B) was amused by the burnt rice
    C) thought her grandmother was extremely silly
    D) truly enjoyed the food
    E) thought her grandmother's comment was funny

21. From this passage, we can assume that the author's family will
    A) keep eating white rice
    B) ban the author from future family meetings
    C) not invite the author for future meals
    D) be very angry and bitter at the author
    E) never try brown rice again

I, Charlotte King, moved to New York from Haiti when I was ten years old. I didn't know an ounce of English. I attended a school full of Haitians who came here recently just like me. I never told my mother that I hated the school: it was as if I had never left Haiti. All the lessons were in French, except for one English class.

Line 5

When my mother came home from work, she made me read out loud from the English textbooks. The first time I tried to read, I sounded like rocks falling in a stream. Then, very slowly, the words started flowing out of my mouth a bit faster. There were words that I heard often like TV, building, and feeling. Eventually, I began to read better. I answered swiftly when my mother asked me a question in English.

10

"Charlotte, you must study hard for the long-term goal," my mother would say. I spent six years doing nothing but that: school, home, and prayer.

15

And then, I fell in love with a boy. He broke the stillness of my life when he moved next door. He had big, brown eyes and skin to match.

22. When Charlotte moved to the United States, she knew

Ⓐ some English
Ⓑ basic English phrases and greetings
Ⓒ conversational English
Ⓓ almost no English
Ⓔ the geography of the United States

23. Charlotte hated her school because

Ⓐ she was bullied for not knowing English
Ⓑ it reminded her of her old neighborhood
Ⓒ the homework was too hard
Ⓓ most classes were taught in French
Ⓔ the teachers were too strict

24. "Rocks falling in a stream" (line 9) describes Charlotte's

Ⓐ pronunciation as she reads
Ⓑ way of moving
Ⓒ way of throwing things
Ⓓ complaints
Ⓔ inability to sit still

25. In the second paragraph, Charlotte started to become

    Ⓐ comfortable with New York culture
    Ⓑ interested in English class
    Ⓒ bold and daring to her mother
    Ⓓ better in speaking and reading English
    Ⓔ interested in English books

26. "Swiftly" (line 13) means

    Ⓐ hastily
    Ⓑ directly
    Ⓒ with hesitation
    Ⓓ carelessly
    Ⓔ without any thought

27. Charlotte describes herself in the third paragraph as being

    Ⓐ lazy and care-free
    Ⓑ fierce and selfish
    Ⓒ determined to prove her mom wrong
    Ⓓ very devoted to her duties
    Ⓔ a bad daughter

28. In line 17, "broke the stillness" means that the boy

    Ⓐ made Charlotte be quiet
    Ⓑ charmed Charlotte's mother
    Ⓒ hurt Charlotte emotionally
    Ⓓ made Charlotte's life interesting
    Ⓔ spoke loudly and rudely

SECTION 4
Writing Sample

Look at the picture and tell a story about what happened. Make sure your story includes a beginning, a middle, and an end.

Elementary Level SSAT
Grade 3

Test 2

SECTION 1
30 Questions

Following each problem in this section, there are five suggested answers. Select the best answer from the five choices. You may use the blank space provided to solve the problem.

Sample Question:

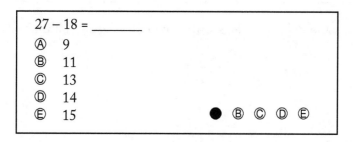

27 – 18 = _____
- Ⓐ 9
- Ⓑ 11
- Ⓒ 13
- Ⓓ 14
- Ⓔ 15

● Ⓑ Ⓒ Ⓓ Ⓔ

---

1. 99 – 4 – 14 =
   - Ⓐ 74
   - Ⓑ 81
   - Ⓒ 84
   - Ⓓ 88
   - Ⓔ 92

---

2. How many inches are there in 5 feet?
   - Ⓐ 5 inches
   - Ⓑ 48 inches
   - Ⓒ 50 inches
   - Ⓓ 60 inches
   - Ⓔ 72 inches

---

3. 2/4 + 1/2
   - Ⓐ 4/4
   - Ⓑ 3/4
   - Ⓒ 2/4
   - Ⓓ 1/4
   - Ⓔ 1/2

4. 42 × 33 =
    Ⓐ 896
    Ⓑ 1,236
    Ⓒ 1,286
    Ⓓ 1,386
    Ⓔ 1,426

---

5. Kenny has 16 cookies and Bobby has 24. How many cookies must Bobby give Kenny if each are to have the same number?
    Ⓐ 2
    Ⓑ 4
    Ⓒ 6
    Ⓓ 8
    Ⓔ 12

---

6. A box holds 8 tennis balls. How many boxes are needed to hold 136 tennis balls?
    Ⓐ 18
    Ⓑ 17
    Ⓒ 16
    Ⓓ 15
    Ⓔ 14

---

7. (7 + 5) ÷ ____ = 2
    Ⓐ 2
    Ⓑ 4
    Ⓒ 6
    Ⓓ 8
    Ⓔ 10

8. Which expression is equal to 720?

   Ⓐ None of these
   Ⓑ 7 × 20
   Ⓒ 8 × 80
   Ⓓ 9 × 80
   Ⓔ 9 × 90

---

9. Which of the following can be drawn without lifting the pencil from the paper and without retracing?

   Ⓐ **A**
   Ⓑ **H**
   Ⓒ **Y**
   Ⓓ **X**
   Ⓔ **P**

---

10. What will be the eighth number in the pattern: 20, 40, 60, 80 ... ?

    Ⓐ 160
    Ⓑ 240
    Ⓒ 320
    Ⓓ 640
    Ⓔ 1,280

---

11. Which two values are located at the same point on a number line?

    Ⓐ 4/1 and 4
    Ⓑ 1/3 and 3
    Ⓒ 2/3 and 3
    Ⓓ 8/8 and 8
    Ⓔ 2/2 and 4

12. How many dimes make up $150?

    Ⓐ 5
    Ⓑ 15
    Ⓒ 150
    Ⓓ 1,500
    Ⓔ 15,000

---

13. 7,000 − ? = 1,899

    Ⓐ 5,101
    Ⓑ 5,100
    Ⓒ 5,099
    Ⓓ 5,090
    Ⓔ 5,089

---

14. If Samuel can run 5 miles in 30 minutes, how many miles can he run in 2 hours?

    Ⓐ 10
    Ⓑ 15
    Ⓒ 20
    Ⓓ 25
    Ⓔ 30

---

15. $\frac{1}{5} + \frac{1}{15} =$

    Ⓐ $\frac{4}{15}$
    Ⓑ $\frac{3}{5}$
    Ⓒ $\frac{3}{15}$
    Ⓓ $\frac{1}{5}$
    Ⓔ $\frac{2}{15}$

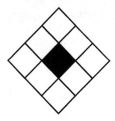

16. What fraction is shaded?

    Ⓐ ⅑
    Ⓑ ⅛
    Ⓒ ⅐
    Ⓓ ⅕
    Ⓔ ¼

17. Mr. Kahn has 152 roses in the beginning of the day. He sold 96 of the roses and then wanted to separate the rest of the roses equally among 8 vases. What is the total number of the roses in one vase?

    Ⓐ 7
    Ⓑ 12
    Ⓒ 14
    Ⓓ 48
    Ⓔ 56

18. Thomas ran around a rectangular field twice. The length of the field is 80 feet and its width is 50 feet. How far did Thomas run?

    Ⓐ 130 feet
    Ⓑ 260 feet
    Ⓒ 460 feet
    Ⓓ 520 feet
    Ⓔ 600 feet

19. A rectangle has a width that is twice that of its length. If the rectangle has a width of 8, what is the area of the rectangle?

    Ⓐ 15 square units
    Ⓑ 20 square units
    Ⓒ 24 square units
    Ⓓ 26 square units
    Ⓔ 32 square units

20. A piece of ribbon 1 meter long is cut into two pieces. One piece is ⅝ m long. What is the length of the other piece?

    Ⓐ ¼ m
    Ⓑ ⅔ m
    Ⓒ ⅜ m
    Ⓓ ⅝ m
    Ⓔ ¾ m

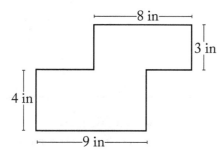

21. What is the total area of the figure?

    Ⓐ 24 square inches
    Ⓑ 48 square inches
    Ⓒ 52 square inches
    Ⓓ 60 square inches
    Ⓔ 72 square inches

22. A machine can fill 150 jars of jam in 10 minutes. How many jars can it fit in 2 hours?

    Ⓐ 1,200
    Ⓑ 1,600
    Ⓒ 1,800
    Ⓓ 2,000
    Ⓔ 2,200

23. What is the 5th number in the sequence: 2, 4, 8...?

    Ⓐ 32
    Ⓑ 30
    Ⓒ 28
    Ⓓ 26
    Ⓔ 24

24. An art lesson started at 5:40 p.m. It lasted 45 minutes. A math lesson started 20 minutes after the art lesson, and lasted 30 minutes. When did the math lesson end?

    Ⓐ 7:15 p.m.
    Ⓑ 7:10 p.m.
    Ⓒ 7:00 p.m.
    Ⓓ 6:55 p.m.
    Ⓔ 6:50 p.m.

25. A triangle has two sides that are equal. One side of the triangle is 5 inches, while another is 4 inches long. What could be the perimeter of the triangle?

    Ⓐ 12 inches
    Ⓑ 14 inches
    Ⓒ 15 inches
    Ⓓ 16 inches
    Ⓔ 17 inches

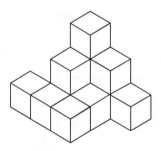

26. How many cubes are in the figure?

    Ⓐ 10
    Ⓑ 12
    Ⓒ 13
    Ⓓ 14
    Ⓔ 15

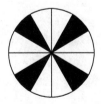

27. What fraction of the figure is shaded?

    Ⓐ 4/15
    Ⓑ 4/16
    Ⓒ ¾
    Ⓓ ⅓
    Ⓔ ⅕

28. A student practices the four musical notes shown on the bottom, starting with the furthest left to the right. If the student plays these notes over and over, and stops immediately after playing the shaded note, which of the following could be the total number of notes played?

    Ⓐ 23
    Ⓑ 22
    Ⓒ 21
    Ⓓ 20
    Ⓔ 18

29. What is the next number in the sequence: 1, 2, 3, 5, 8, 13, 21, 34...

    Ⓐ 55
    Ⓑ 59
    Ⓒ 63
    Ⓓ 71
    Ⓔ 77

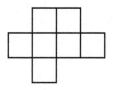

30. How many 4-sided figures are there?

    Ⓐ 14
    Ⓑ 16
    Ⓒ 17
    Ⓓ 18
    Ⓔ 20

SECTION 2
30 Questions

Synonyms
Following each problem in this section, there are five suggested answers. Select the best answer from the five choices. You may use the blank space provided to solve the problem.

Sample Question:

> TIRED:
> Ⓐ sleepy
> Ⓑ sad
> Ⓒ fast
> Ⓓ perky
> Ⓔ hungry
>
> ● Ⓑ Ⓒ Ⓓ Ⓔ

---

1. TIMID
   Ⓐ fancy
   Ⓑ plain
   Ⓒ shy
   Ⓓ yellow
   Ⓔ clever

2. DISCOVER
   Ⓐ burn
   Ⓑ develop
   Ⓒ plan
   Ⓓ show
   Ⓔ locate

3. LOCATE
   Ⓐ show
   Ⓑ use
   Ⓒ find
   Ⓓ trade
   Ⓔ squeeze

4. EXPLORE
   Ⓐ search
   Ⓑ remember
   Ⓒ work
   Ⓓ transport
   Ⓔ remove

5. COURAGEOUS
   Ⓐ protect
   Ⓑ improve
   Ⓒ encourage
   Ⓓ bold
   Ⓔ count

6. PERFORM
   Ⓐ act
   Ⓑ challenge
   Ⓒ forgive
   Ⓓ argue
   Ⓔ build

7. MISERY
   Ⓐ map
   Ⓑ hardship
   Ⓒ problem
   Ⓓ month
   Ⓔ failure

8. EXAMINE
   Ⓐ analyze
   Ⓑ introduce
   Ⓒ dust
   Ⓓ ask
   Ⓔ guide

9. THEORY
   - Ⓐ math
   - Ⓑ skill
   - Ⓒ teacher
   - Ⓓ beginning
   - Ⓔ idea

10. PRIMARY
    - Ⓐ ugly
    - Ⓑ main
    - Ⓒ important
    - Ⓓ wrong
    - Ⓔ scary

11. FLATTER
    - Ⓐ head
    - Ⓑ multiply
    - Ⓒ attract
    - Ⓓ dislike
    - Ⓔ charm

12. AMBITION
    - Ⓐ desire
    - Ⓑ side
    - Ⓒ question
    - Ⓓ trouble
    - Ⓔ confidence

13. RESTRICT
    - Ⓐ correct
    - Ⓑ limit
    - Ⓒ dress
    - Ⓓ guide
    - Ⓔ keep

14. WISDOM
    - Ⓐ doctor
    - Ⓑ mouth
    - Ⓒ highlight
    - Ⓓ knowledge
    - Ⓔ information

15. SALVAGE
    - Ⓐ find
    - Ⓑ recycle
    - Ⓒ exercise
    - Ⓓ damage
    - Ⓔ connect

Analogies

Following each problem in this section, there are five suggested answers. Select the best answer from the five choices. You may use the blank space provided to solve the problem.

Sample Question:

> Song is to composer as
> Ⓐ book is to author
> Ⓑ clay is to sculptor
> Ⓒ hammer is to carpenter
> Ⓓ script is to actor
> Ⓔ microphone is to singer   ● Ⓑ Ⓒ Ⓓ Ⓔ

Choice Ⓐ is the best answer because a song is written by a composer, just as a book is written by an author. Of all the answer choices, Ⓐ states a relationship that is most like the relationship between song and composer.

---

16. Pillow is to bed as cushion is to
    Ⓐ table
    Ⓑ desk
    Ⓒ tub
    Ⓓ sink
    Ⓔ chair

17. Moon is to evening as sun is to
    Ⓐ midnight
    Ⓑ noon
    Ⓒ morning
    Ⓓ solar system
    Ⓔ summer

18. Fast is to swift as tired is to
    Ⓐ hasty
    Ⓑ confused
    Ⓒ exhausted
    Ⓓ nervous
    Ⓔ happy

19. Carpenter is to hammer as painter is to
    Ⓐ ink
    Ⓑ brush
    Ⓒ canvas
    Ⓓ mask
    Ⓔ wood

20. Hiking is to mountain as surfing is to
    Ⓐ ocean
    Ⓑ breeze
    Ⓒ sand
    Ⓓ pool
    Ⓔ water

21. Cookie is to bake as coffee is to
    Ⓐ drink
    Ⓑ cook
    Ⓒ swirl
    Ⓓ brew
    Ⓔ heat

22. happy is to giggle as sad is to
    Ⓐ frown
    Ⓑ sleep
    Ⓒ watch
    Ⓓ pant
    Ⓔ scream

23. Tennis is to court as soccer is to
    Ⓐ grass
    Ⓑ ball
    Ⓒ diamond
    Ⓓ field
    Ⓔ net

24. Flower is to rose as mammal is to
    Ⓐ lizard
    Ⓑ bear
    Ⓒ fur
    Ⓓ pet
    Ⓔ farm

25. Violin is to bow as drum is to
    Ⓐ stage
    Ⓑ stick
    Ⓒ trombone
    Ⓓ gong
    Ⓔ drummer

26. Summary is to story as abbreviation is to
    Ⓐ letter
    Ⓑ word
    Ⓒ chapter
    Ⓓ letter
    Ⓔ marking

27. tree is to bark as person is to
    Ⓐ skin
    Ⓑ job
    Ⓒ face
    Ⓓ bone
    Ⓔ clothes

28. Instruct is to teacher as protect is to
    Ⓐ principal
    Ⓑ lawyer
    Ⓒ janitor
    Ⓓ nurse
    Ⓔ goalie

29. Square is to cube as circle is to
    Ⓐ ball
    Ⓑ round
    Ⓒ triangle
    Ⓓ sphere
    Ⓔ oval

30. Collar is to shirt as cuff is to
    Ⓐ pants
    Ⓑ tie
    Ⓒ leg
    Ⓓ socks
    Ⓔ sweater

SECTION 3
28 QUESTIONS

Read each passage carefully and then answer the questions about it. For each question, decide on the basis of the passage which one of the choices best answers the questions.

> All matter is made up of atoms. Different kinds of atoms can combine to form new substances. This page you are reading is made up of millions and millions of atoms. So are you!
>
> Line 5   An atom is an exceedingly small thing. For example, it would take a line of about 200 million hydrogen atoms, the smallest kind of atoms, to measure up to a distance of one inch.
>
> In the nineteenth century, many great thinkers and
> 10   minds thought that atoms were invisible blobs of matter. Now we know that atoms are far more complicated. We also know that under the right conditions certain atoms can be split into smaller things. When this happens, energy is given off. Sometimes, it is possible to capture this energy in the form of
> 15   heat. We can then convert this heat to make electricity.

1. We can assume that animals
    - (A) are not matter
    - (B) give off energy
    - (C) are made up of atoms
    - (D) create matter
    - (E) eat atoms

2. What does the word "exceedingly" in line 5 mean?
    - (A) unexpectedly
    - (B) fortunately
    - (C) increasingly
    - (D) very
    - (E) somewhat

3. We can assume that atoms are
    - (A) invisible to the human eye
    - (B) very heavy
    - (C) metallic in taste
    - (D) poisonous
    - (E) bright and shiny

4. The author thinks the great thinkers and minds of the nineteenth century were _____ in their view of atoms.
    - (A) foolish and arrogant
    - (B) extremely smart and geniuses
    - (C) totally right
    - (D) clueless
    - (E) generally correct

5. The energy given off by splitting atoms is
   Ⓐ heat
   Ⓑ light
   Ⓒ invisible
   Ⓓ enormous
   Ⓔ magic

6. What does the word "convert" in line 15 mean?
   Ⓐ spark
   Ⓑ change
   Ⓒ twist
   Ⓓ build
   Ⓔ flame

7. The main idea of the passage is
   Ⓐ how matter is made
   Ⓑ how to create electricity
   Ⓒ atomic heat system
   Ⓓ what atoms are like
   Ⓔ nineteenth century discoveries

In ancient Botswana, Chief Kahli ruled all creatures. Chief Kahli loved parties and festivals so he invited subjects to feast with him and give speeches.

One night, the final speaker to address the crowd was
Line 5 ant. Though tiny, he spoke boldly. "My kind is stronger than any other," he claimed. "No creature, from the slimy, wriggling worm to the mighty bush elephant, can withstand us!"

The worms at the feast took great offense at the driver ant's insults and boasts. They complained bitterly to Chief
10 Kahli. "There is but one way to settle this matter," Kahli said. "Both sides shall meet in my great field in three days. There and then, you shall settle this matter." Both sides agreed.

Three days later, a hundred thousand ants marched together toward Kahli's field, like a rippling brown carpet.
15 Scout ants led the way and guard ants kept the others in tight formation.

When the ants reached the field, they spotted the worms slithering in anticipation. Suddenly the carpet came undone. Each ant rolled into a tiny ball, and they
20 overwhelmed the sluggish worms from every side. The contest was over in moments. The defeated worms slithered away and buried themselves out of sight to tend their wounds.

8. Chief Kahli in the first paragraph is described as
   - Ⓐ mean-spirited
   - Ⓑ intelligent
   - Ⓒ fun-loving
   - Ⓓ lazy
   - Ⓔ hard-working

9. What was the result of the ant's speech in paragraph 2?
   - Ⓐ Creatures began to leave.
   - Ⓑ Creatures began rioting.
   - Ⓒ Chief Kahli was impressed by the ant's speech.
   - Ⓓ Feelings were hurt.
   - Ⓔ Another party was planned.

10. The ants in paragraph 2 are best described as
    - Ⓐ bold and kind
    - Ⓑ daring and fearless
    - Ⓒ cruel and devious
    - Ⓓ respectful and humble
    - Ⓔ confident and cheerful

11. What does Chief Kahli do after the worms complain?
    - Ⓐ He comforts them.
    - Ⓑ He plans another feast.
    - Ⓒ He ignores them.
    - Ⓓ He proposes a solution.
    - Ⓔ He looks down on them.

12. The marching ants are described as "a rippling brown carpet" to describe their
    Ⓐ uniforms
    Ⓑ movement
    Ⓒ bravery
    Ⓓ weapons
    Ⓔ hunger

13. The guard ants were probably marching _____ of the formation.
    Ⓐ by the sides
    Ⓑ on the bottom
    Ⓒ at the front
    Ⓓ on top
    Ⓔ in the center

14. The ants attacked the worm by
    Ⓐ remaining in formation
    Ⓑ separating and swarming
    Ⓒ coming from three directions
    Ⓓ surprising the enemy
    Ⓔ yelling and charging

Valeria the fox felt and heard her empty stomach growl. She hadn't eaten anything in days. The field mice were too quick, and the rabbits stayed well hidden in the brush. Valeria couldn't even manage to snag a plump hen from the local farm or drag a delicious duck from a pond.

One desperate night, she stumbled upon a lush garden one night and took a sniff. A sweet and juicy scent filled her nose, and Valeria gazed up. She saw a vine with a bunch of deep purple grapes. Valeria stared longingly at the bursting bunches, so ripe and ready to be devoured.

Valeria stretched her body upward and scaled the vine. But the grapes hung too high up, beyond her reach. After many attempts of climbing, she tried to leap as high into the air as she could. Again and again, she leapt but even the lowest branch was out of her reach. She even tried to throw rocks at the bunches to whack them loose. But the grapes stubbornly hung high and proudly.

Valeria was too weary to jump, throw or climb any more. She hung her tails and slouched over. After a minute of moping, she shouted, "Oh you miserable grapes! Who wants to eat sour grapes anyway?"

15. Field mice and rabbits are Valeria's
    - Ⓐ enemy
    - Ⓑ friends
    - Ⓒ favorite meal
    - Ⓓ prey
    - Ⓔ hunters

16. Valeria's main problem in the first paragraph was that she
    - Ⓐ didn't know where to rest
    - Ⓑ was angry at the farmer
    - Ⓒ couldn't outrun the rabbits
    - Ⓓ was starving
    - Ⓔ was too tired to hunt

17. The phrase "One desperate night" (line 6) suggests that Valeria is
    - Ⓐ cursing her fate
    - Ⓑ giving up searching for food
    - Ⓒ running out of options
    - Ⓓ looking for protection
    - Ⓔ losing her mind

18. What does the word "longingly" (line 9) mean?
    - Ⓐ intensely
    - Ⓑ smartly
    - Ⓒ lovingly
    - Ⓓ quickly
    - Ⓔ jealously

19. What does the word "attempts" (line 13) mean?

    Ⓐ twirls
    Ⓑ rounds
    Ⓒ plans
    Ⓓ rolls
    Ⓔ tails

20. What does it mean that the grapes stubbornly hung high and proudly?

    Ⓐ the grapes made fun of Valeria
    Ⓑ the grapes were about to fall
    Ⓒ the grapes had a strong personality
    Ⓓ the grapes were determined to hang on
    Ⓔ the grapes wouldn't budge

21. Valeria's last comments tells us that she is

    Ⓐ bitter at her failures
    Ⓑ angry for being hungry
    Ⓒ wise in her guess that the grapes are sour
    Ⓓ not hungry anymore
    Ⓔ determined to improve herself later on

Television has always had a bad reputation. People would lambaste it, warning the public about its evils. This is nothing new, of course, and as the years pass, this negative emotion doesn't appear to go away.

I think that a lot of people fear and hate television because it is so popular. Television has been blamed for corrupting our young, and exciting our adults by presenting a false view of the world. But is television really capable of such evil deeds? Before TV, radio and movies were accused of the same thing. And even longer before that, philosophers were warning their citizens of the corrupting power of poetry and drama.

Even Plato, a famous philosopher in ancient Greece, stated that "poetry is not to be taken seriously." He did not like that characters in poetry were overly emotional. He preferred serious discussions rather than exaggerated phrases.

But some historians have said that Plato and other philosophers were just elitists. The philosophers stuck their nose at the common people. Perhaps television is suffering the same fate as poetry and drama did back in the days.

22. What does the word "lambaste" mean in line 2?
   A attack
   B support
   C question
   D subtract
   E defend

23. The first paragraph describes the negative emotion towards television as
   A ridiculous
   B weird
   C confusing
   D lasting
   E evil

24. We can tell from the second paragraph that the author
   A thinks television may not be as harmful
   B secretly hates television and its effects
   C owns many television sets
   D supports the popularity of televisions
   E secretly loves to watch television

25. The author mentions poetry and drama in the second paragraph because they
   A were attacked for being harmful
   B are more educational than television
   C were loved by the Greeks
   D were philosopher's favorite genres
   E were as popular as television

26. The third paragraph suggests that Plato did not like poetry because it was
    - Ⓐ too interesting
    - Ⓑ too boring
    - Ⓒ too serious
    - Ⓓ too dramatic
    - Ⓔ too complicated

27. "Elitist" (line 18) can be best described as
    - Ⓐ snobby
    - Ⓑ secretive
    - Ⓒ weak
    - Ⓓ smart
    - Ⓔ rich

28. The main purpose of this passage is to
    - Ⓐ give a possible reason for television's bad reputation
    - Ⓑ tell a personal story of poetry's wonders
    - Ⓒ attack the ancient philosophers' ideas
    - Ⓓ describe television's rise in popularity
    - Ⓔ support the freedom to watch television

SECTION 4
Writing Sample

Look at the picture and tell a story about what happened. Make sure your story includes a beginning, a middle, and an end.

Elementary Level SSAT
Grade 3

Test 3

SECTION 1
30 Questions

Following each problem in this section, there are five suggested answers. Select the best answer from the five choices. You may use the blank space provided to solve the problem.

Sample Question:

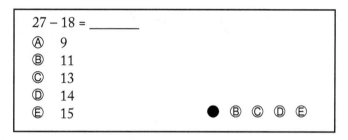

1. 99 + 999 =

    Ⓐ 108
    Ⓑ 1,000
    Ⓒ 1,008
    Ⓓ 1,098
    Ⓔ 1,198

2. Marjorie has 78 plates to pack into moving boxes. Each box holds 4 plates. How many boxes does she need to pack all 78 plates?

    Ⓐ 12
    Ⓑ 15
    Ⓒ 18
    Ⓓ 19
    Ⓔ 20

3. Which is the biggest fraction?

    Ⓐ $\frac{1}{2}$

    Ⓑ $\frac{1}{3}$

    Ⓒ $\frac{1}{5}$

    Ⓓ $\frac{1}{25}$

    Ⓔ $\frac{1}{30}$

4. ⅓ + ⅔ =
   - Ⓐ ½
   - Ⓑ 1
   - Ⓒ 2
   - Ⓓ 3
   - Ⓔ 5

5. Jake is 5 years old, and Jessica is 3 years older than Jake. In 12 years, how old will Jessica be?
   - Ⓐ 20
   - Ⓑ 19
   - Ⓒ 18
   - Ⓓ 14
   - Ⓔ 12

6. There are 4 cups to a quart, and 4 quarts to a gallon. How many cups are there in 1 gallon?
   - Ⓐ 4
   - Ⓑ 8
   - Ⓒ 12
   - Ⓓ 16
   - Ⓔ 20

7. What is the perimeter of a rectangle with length of 1 and width of ½?
   - Ⓐ 3
   - Ⓑ 4
   - Ⓒ 6
   - Ⓓ 9
   - Ⓔ 12

8. 2/4 + 5/12

    Ⓐ 7/24
    Ⓑ 6/14
    Ⓒ 7/16
    Ⓓ 7/12
    Ⓔ 11/12

9. A piece of blue ribbon is 2 feet 4 inches long. A piece of yellow ribbon is 2 feet and 8 inches. What is the total length of the blue and yellow ribbons?

    Ⓐ 4 feet
    Ⓑ 4 feet 2 inches
    Ⓒ 4 feet 6 inches
    Ⓓ 4 feet 8 inches
    Ⓔ 5 feet

10. On a map, ½ inch represents 3 yards. If I measure 2 inches on the map, how far is that in yards?

    Ⓐ 6
    Ⓑ 8
    Ⓒ 10
    Ⓓ 12
    Ⓔ 14

11. Joanne ran 2 miles on Monday, Wednesday, and Thursday, and 3 miles on Tuesday and Friday. She rested on the weekends. If she keeps up this exact schedule, how many miles will she run in 5 weeks?

    Ⓐ 12
    Ⓑ 24
    Ⓒ 48
    Ⓓ 60
    Ⓔ 75

12. 12 − 7 + ? = 22
    Ⓐ 12
    Ⓑ 15
    Ⓒ 17
    Ⓓ 20
    Ⓔ 21

13. Which of the following statement is true?
    Ⓐ ½ > ⅔
    Ⓑ ⅚ < ⅜
    Ⓒ ¼ > ⅓
    Ⓓ ¹⁄₁₀ < 0
    Ⓔ None of the above

14. 3 is to 15 as 4 is to ____
    Ⓐ 16
    Ⓑ 18
    Ⓒ 20
    Ⓓ 22
    Ⓔ 24

15. 20 quarters is the same as
    Ⓐ 20 dollars
    Ⓑ 100 nickels
    Ⓒ 60 dimes
    Ⓓ 2 quarters and 50 nickels
    Ⓔ 2 dollars and 20 dimes

16. If two times a number is 6 less than 42, what is the number?
    - Ⓐ 16
    - Ⓑ 18
    - Ⓒ 22
    - Ⓓ 24
    - Ⓔ 28

---

17. $3 \times 4 \times \,? = 6 \times 2$
    - Ⓐ 0
    - Ⓑ 1
    - Ⓒ 2
    - Ⓓ 4
    - Ⓔ 6

---

18. If the perimeter of a rectangle is 20, and the width is 4, what is the length?
    - Ⓐ 4
    - Ⓑ 6
    - Ⓒ 10
    - Ⓓ 12
    - Ⓔ 20

---

19. A rope measuring 120 inches is divided into 3 equal parts. One of the part of the rope is then divided into 5 equal parts. What is the length of one of the smallest piece?
    - Ⓐ 8 inches
    - Ⓑ 10 inches
    - Ⓒ 12 inches
    - Ⓓ 20 inches
    - Ⓔ 40 inches

20. Eduardo wants to place a ribbon on each chair of is 27 grandchildren attending the family dinner. There are 4 balloons in each package. How many packages must he buy?
    - Ⓐ 5
    - Ⓑ 6
    - Ⓒ 7
    - Ⓓ 9
    - Ⓔ 11

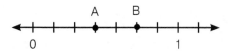

21. What is the value midway between point A and point B?
    - Ⓐ 3/7
    - Ⓑ 4/7
    - Ⓒ 5/7
    - Ⓓ 6/7
    - Ⓔ 7/7

22. A river is 14 inches below flood stage at 1 p.m. If it rises 36 inches by 7 p.m., then the river will be
    - Ⓐ 22 inches below flood stage
    - Ⓑ 22 inches above flood stage
    - Ⓒ 16 inches below flood stage
    - Ⓓ 44 inches above flood stage
    - Ⓔ 50 inches above flood stage

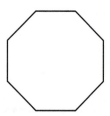

23. How many angles are there in the figure?
    - Ⓐ 6
    - Ⓑ 7
    - Ⓒ 8
    - Ⓓ 9
    - Ⓔ 10

24. If Cathy gets paid $15 after every hour worked, how many hours must she work to earn more than $302?

    Ⓐ 10
    Ⓑ 11
    Ⓒ 18
    Ⓓ 20
    Ⓔ 21

---

25. 1 – ⅖ – ³⁄₃₀ =

    Ⓐ ½
    Ⓑ ⅖
    Ⓒ ⁸⁄₁₅
    Ⓓ ⅗
    Ⓔ ²¹⁄₃₀

---

26. The sides of a square with perimeter 8 inches is doubled. What is the area of the new square?

    Ⓐ 8 square inches
    Ⓑ 12 square inches
    Ⓒ 16 square inches
    Ⓓ 20 square inches
    Ⓔ 24 square inches

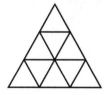

27. How many triangles are there?

    Ⓐ 9
    Ⓑ 10
    Ⓒ 11
    Ⓓ 12
    Ⓔ 14

28. A piece of yellow tape is 5 feet and 4 inches long. A piece of red tape is 2 feet and 8 inches shorter. What is the total length of the yellow and red tapes in inches?

    Ⓐ 62
    Ⓑ 78
    Ⓒ 88
    Ⓓ 92
    Ⓔ 96

29. The capacity of a tank is 18 and a half gallons. How many quarts of water can it hold? Note: 4 quarts = 1 gallon.

    Ⓐ 72
    Ⓑ 74
    Ⓒ 76
    Ⓓ 78
    Ⓔ 80

30. What is a number that can be divided evenly by 3, 5 and 7?

    Ⓐ 300
    Ⓑ 455
    Ⓒ 575
    Ⓓ 630
    Ⓔ 665

SECTION 2
30 Questions

Synonyms
Following each problem in this section, there are five suggested answers. Select the best answer from the five choices. You may use the blank space provided to solve the problem.

Sample Question:

> TIRED:
> Ⓐ sleepy
> Ⓑ sad
> Ⓒ fast
> Ⓓ perky
> Ⓔ hungry
>
> ● Ⓑ Ⓒ Ⓓ Ⓔ

---

1. AVOID
   Ⓐ accept
   Ⓑ play
   Ⓒ escape
   Ⓓ use
   Ⓔ divide

2. JOURNEY
   Ⓐ bird
   Ⓑ travel
   Ⓒ direction
   Ⓓ energy
   Ⓔ world

3. REMARK
   Ⓐ pet
   Ⓑ comment
   Ⓒ learn
   Ⓓ introduce
   Ⓔ hear

4. ORIGIN
   Ⓐ root
   Ⓑ freedom
   Ⓒ lake
   Ⓓ growth
   Ⓔ family

5. PLUNGE
   Ⓐ fall
   Ⓑ comfort
   Ⓒ grab
   Ⓓ kneel
   Ⓔ leave

6. DEFEND
   Ⓐ ice
   Ⓑ demand
   Ⓒ beg
   Ⓓ guard
   Ⓔ answer

7. HABIT
   Ⓐ attention
   Ⓑ wood
   Ⓒ routine
   Ⓓ system
   Ⓔ owner

8. REVEAL
   Ⓐ brush
   Ⓑ bend
   Ⓒ judge
   Ⓓ show
   Ⓔ end

63

9. CLIMATE
   - Ⓐ virus
   - Ⓑ actor
   - Ⓒ temperature
   - Ⓓ country
   - Ⓔ environment

10. PREDATOR
    - Ⓐ thought
    - Ⓑ army
    - Ⓒ camera
    - Ⓓ member
    - Ⓔ hunter

11. IMITATE
    - Ⓐ grip
    - Ⓑ copy
    - Ⓒ impress
    - Ⓓ join
    - Ⓔ produce

12. ORDEAL
    - Ⓐ length
    - Ⓑ failure
    - Ⓒ discussion
    - Ⓓ criticism
    - Ⓔ hardship

13. WOE
    - Ⓐ sorrow
    - Ⓑ memory
    - Ⓒ drama
    - Ⓓ win
    - Ⓔ problem

14. METHOD
    - Ⓐ elevator
    - Ⓑ guest
    - Ⓒ sample
    - Ⓓ technique
    - Ⓔ information

15. PRIVILEGE
    - Ⓐ health
    - Ⓑ opportunity
    - Ⓒ problem
    - Ⓓ understanding
    - Ⓔ activity

Analogies

Following each problem in this section, there are five suggested answers. Select the best answer from the five choices. You may use the blank space provided to solve the problem.

Sample Question:

> Song is to composer as
> Ⓐ book is to author
> Ⓑ clay is to sculptor
> Ⓒ hammer is to carpenter
> Ⓓ script is to actor
> Ⓔ microphone is to singer
>
> ● Ⓑ Ⓒ Ⓓ Ⓔ

Choice Ⓐ is the best answer because a song is written by a composer, just as a book is written by an author. Of all the answer choices, Ⓐ states a relationship that is most like the relationship between song and composer.

---

16. sharp is to dull as fast is to
    Ⓐ blunt
    Ⓑ quick
    Ⓒ slow
    Ⓓ pointed
    Ⓔ lazy

17. run is to jog as walk is to
    Ⓐ sprint
    Ⓑ talk
    Ⓒ hurry
    Ⓓ stroll
    Ⓔ turn

18. ball is to round as stick is to
    Ⓐ hard
    Ⓑ wooden
    Ⓒ sharp
    Ⓓ long
    Ⓔ shiny

19. petal is to flower as leaf is to
    Ⓐ fall
    Ⓑ bark
    Ⓒ wood
    Ⓓ tree
    Ⓔ health

20. nose is to face as tooth is to
    Ⓐ nail
    Ⓑ mouth
    Ⓒ ache
    Ⓓ brush
    Ⓔ tongue

21. insect is to ladybug as trout is to
    Ⓐ swim
    Ⓑ water
    Ⓒ fish
    Ⓓ whale
    Ⓔ tuna

22. plane is to pilot as train is to
    Ⓐ wheel
    Ⓑ conductor
    Ⓒ passenger
    Ⓓ station
    Ⓔ instructor

23. waiter is to restaurant as secretary is to
    Ⓐ pool
    Ⓑ business
    Ⓒ park
    Ⓓ office
    Ⓔ job

24. tub is to ice-cream as gallon is to
    Ⓐ carrot
    Ⓑ chocolate
    Ⓒ milk
    Ⓓ dust
    Ⓔ ticket

25. tornado is to destruction as medicine is to
    Ⓐ sickness
    Ⓑ hospital
    Ⓒ doctor
    Ⓓ healing
    Ⓔ price

26. seal is to sea as hawk is to
    Ⓐ mountain
    Ⓑ nest
    Ⓒ ocean
    Ⓓ sky
    Ⓔ oxygen

27. chain is to metal as ribbon is to
    Ⓐ dress
    Ⓑ tie
    Ⓒ cloth
    Ⓓ sleeve
    Ⓔ pearl

28. exercise is to gym as eat is to
    Ⓐ food
    Ⓑ store
    Ⓒ cafeteria
    Ⓓ park
    Ⓔ plate

29. spring is to blossom as autumn is to
    Ⓐ blow
    Ⓑ relax
    Ⓒ grow
    Ⓓ thank
    Ⓔ wither

30. Burnt is to toast as rot is to
    Ⓐ child
    Ⓑ garbage
    Ⓒ dessert
    Ⓓ meat
    Ⓔ rust

SECTION 3
28 QUESTIONS

Read each passage carefully and then answer the questions about it. For each question, decide on the basis of the passage which one of the choices best answers the questions.

> My eyelids feel heavy and they begin to droop
> My head bobs and my thoughts become loose
> As I lie down on the bed
> With the fresh coldness of the untouched blanket
> Line 5   It looks so inviting as if it were calling me
>
> But I know better;
> There is no such thing as a tranquil pause
> How many more restless night must I suffer
> When I will twist and turn
> 10   But then, before I know it, my eyes open—
> The sun has risen!
>
> I must have slept through the dark night,
> The day is in front of me
> Filled with hope and possibility
> 15   The roads suddenly widen,
> Broad enough to encompass all of my intentions

1. What does it mean for thoughts to become loose?

    Ⓐ You can't remember your childhood
    Ⓑ You start imagining things
    Ⓒ You become more hungry
    Ⓓ You can't think clearly
    Ⓔ You start shivering in madness

2. We can infer that the blanket is cold because

    Ⓐ the air-conditioner is on
    Ⓑ it is lonely
    Ⓒ the room is chilly
    Ⓓ it is winter
    Ⓔ the windows are probably open

3. What does the word "tranquil" (line 7) mean?

    Ⓐ peaceful
    Ⓑ fearful
    Ⓒ final
    Ⓓ forever
    Ⓔ shocking

4. Line 6 suggests that sleep

    Ⓐ is a moment away
    Ⓑ is a good idea
    Ⓒ is very bad for your health
    Ⓓ is not relaxing for the author
    Ⓔ is never surprising

5. What happens in lines 10-11?
   - Ⓐ The author fumbles in bed
   - Ⓑ The author wakes up in the morning
   - Ⓒ The sun shines through the window
   - Ⓓ The author sleeps when the sun rises
   - Ⓔ The author has another nightmare

6. The main problem described in the poem is the author
   - Ⓐ has terrifying nightmares
   - Ⓑ cannot find a good place to sleep
   - Ⓒ is too tired to think logically
   - Ⓓ is too cold and uncomfortable
   - Ⓔ has trouble getting good sleep

7. The poem ends with a tone of
   - Ⓐ regret
   - Ⓑ fear
   - Ⓒ confusion
   - Ⓓ frustration
   - Ⓔ hope

Line 5

Hundreds of years ago, people tried to change metal into gold. Alchemy is the name given to this endeavor. Today, alchemy is considered a sham, a hoax. No one really takes it seriously. It is often called a pseudoscience–something mistakenly regarded as scientific.

But for many centuries, alchemy was a respected art. The alchemists were obsessed with dreams of impossible wealth. Alchemists helped developed many steps and procedures that present-day scientists follow, especially in chemistry. Although the alchemists never successfully changed lead into gold, their gift to us was far greater.

In fact, during the Scientific Revolution, many scientists relied on all the observations and data that the alchemists collected. Most alchemists were very organized and detailed. As society moved on from alchemy to modern science, the tales of alchemists sitting in front of a huge cauldron stirring stuck with the public's imagination. Some laughed at the absurd situation while others mocked the idea. But one thing was for sure: alchemy forever earned its place in history.

8. What does the word "endeavor" in line 2 mean?

Ⓐ attempt
Ⓑ experience
Ⓒ instruction
Ⓓ science
Ⓔ magic

9. The words "sham" and "hoax" in line 3 suggests that alchemy is now considered

Ⓐ with respect
Ⓑ scientific
Ⓒ as fake
Ⓓ complicated
Ⓔ possible

10. People tried changing metals into gold because

Ⓐ they wanted to get richer
Ⓑ they were curious about the natural world
Ⓒ they cared about scientific principles
Ⓓ they were fascinated by metal
Ⓔ they wanted fame and respect

11. What might be an example of "their gift to us" in lines 10-11?

Ⓐ diary accounts of alchemists' hopes
Ⓑ tools that help store gold
Ⓒ scientific properties of metals
Ⓓ instructions on how to change lead into gold
Ⓔ scientific discoveries of chemical compounds

12. The author views alchemy and alchemists with
    Ⓐ sudden shock and suspicion
    Ⓑ bitter disappointment
    Ⓒ soft love and joy
    Ⓓ extreme respect and admiration
    Ⓔ some interest and curiosity

13. The author of the passage would agree that
    Ⓐ metals can turn into gold
    Ⓑ alchemists were junior scientists
    Ⓒ chemistry is the most important subject
    Ⓓ people are cruel to laugh at alchemy
    Ⓔ alchemy was once considered possible

14. The style of the passage is most like that found in a
    Ⓐ a scientist's diary
    Ⓑ novel about alchemists
    Ⓒ history textbook
    Ⓓ newspaper article
    Ⓔ personal letter

The Ancient Greeks believed that everything should be done in the right amount. Even too much exercise can be bad for your health.

Line 5 The holidays are a great time to celebrate and bond with family. However, during these times, most people tend to overeat and drink and pack on the pounds. This is followed by a nationwide fitness craze. People sign up for gyms, programs and buy exercise equipments that they end up never using. However, health experts are warning people to not go on an
10 "exercise craze" which can lead to injuries and disappointment.

Over-exercising can damage muscles and bones. For example, bones can suffer from microscopic fractures from repeated exercise. Bones need time to adapt to new movements, so people should gradually increase the length
15 and intensity of the exercise.

Moderate exercise, which leaves you slightly breathless, is recommended by most experts. This includes brisk walking, cycling, and even gardening.

You cannot expect to reverse the harmful effects of
20 overeating in one day or even one week. The best way to not injure yourself is to take it slowly, one day at a time, one exercise at a time.

15. The Ancient Greeks considered exercise as
    A silly
    B tiresome
    C necessary
    D poisonous
    E none of the above

16. According to the author, the holidays are
    A times when people don't eat much
    B too long and drawn-out
    C time to connect with loved ones
    D harmful because people don't exercise
    E mostly boring and dull

17. Why do people go on a nationwide fitness craze after the holidays?
    A They want to lose the weight gained from the holidays
    B They want to feel less full from the holiday feasts
    C They want to look better for spring
    D They are bored of relaxing and want to move around
    E They feel guilty for not eating and drinking more

18. Health experts view fitness craze with
    A disappointment
    B happiness
    C frustration
    D caution
    E anger

19. What does the word "gradually" (line 14) mean?
    Ⓐ painfully
    Ⓑ carelessly
    Ⓒ slowly
    Ⓓ logically
    Ⓔ swiftly

20. Which of the following can be considered moderate exercise?
    Ⓐ jumping jacks
    Ⓑ sprinting
    Ⓒ bathing
    Ⓓ sleeping
    Ⓔ heavy weightlifting

21. The tone of this passage is best described as
    Ⓐ defensive
    Ⓑ instructive
    Ⓒ encouraging
    Ⓓ chatty
    Ⓔ harsh

On May 18, 1980, Mount Saint Helens erupted. A cloud of dust blanketed the sky, spreading fifteen miles into the air. The explosion was not a surprise because the earth's crust had shaken for weeks beforehand. People had plenty of
Line 5   advance warning.

Despite these danger signals, no one was prepared for how severe the blast was. Over the course of several weeks, the volcano's eruption ripped the top 1,300 feet off the mountain. This resulted in a landslide that was the largest in recorded
10   history. Around 500 million tons of ash from the volcano were spread over three states. The earth's weather pattern was even affected for several years afterward!

The initial volcanic eruption was missing one thing: lava. Later eruptions spewed out a thick and oozing lava. Thick
15   lava is easily outrun because it moves extremely slowly. In addition, thick lava often cools and hardens near the eruption zone, making the volcanic mountains "taller." However, Mount Saint Helens never produced enough lava. It became much "shorter" after the fateful explosion.

22. What does the word "blanketed" mean in line 2?
    Ⓐ covered
    Ⓑ twisted
    Ⓒ hugged
    Ⓓ darkened
    Ⓔ wrapped

23. What does the word "advance" mean in line 5?
    Ⓐ urgent
    Ⓑ in the past
    Ⓒ undetected
    Ⓓ moving forward
    Ⓔ ahead of time

24. What might be an example of the "danger signals" in line 6?
    Ⓐ tremors
    Ⓑ longer nights
    Ⓒ strong winds
    Ⓓ fog
    Ⓔ forest fires

25. The main purpose of the second paragraph is to
    Ⓐ shock and scare the readers
    Ⓑ warn the readers of natural disasters
    Ⓒ describe the extreme impact of the eruption
    Ⓓ point out the expert's failures in warning the public
    Ⓔ inform the readers on the dangers of volcanoes

26. The exclamation mark in line 12 suggests the author's _____
    - Ⓐ confusion
    - Ⓑ fear
    - Ⓒ playfulness
    - Ⓓ joy
    - Ⓔ awe

27. What does the word "initial" mean in line 13?
    - Ⓐ important
    - Ⓑ second
    - Ⓒ biggest
    - Ⓓ first
    - Ⓔ last

28. It can be inferred that today, Mount Saint Helens
    - Ⓐ is feared and hated by many people
    - Ⓑ has many different wildlife
    - Ⓒ does not have a pointed peak
    - Ⓓ is the most popular tourist site
    - Ⓔ has dark soil and few trees

SECTION 4
Writing Sample

Look at the picture and tell a story about what happened. Make sure your story includes a beginning, a middle, and an end.

Answer Key

Test 1   Answer Key

Section 1: Quantitative		Section 2: Verbal		Section 3: Reading	
Question	Answer	Question	Answer	Question	Answer
1	A	1	B	1	C
2	D	2	B	2	E
3	E	3	D	3	D
4	C	4	C	4	B
5	D	5	E	5	B
6	E	6	E	6	E
7	E	7	A	7	D
8	D	8	E	8	D
9	B	9	B	9	E
10	D	10	A	10	D
11	D	11	D	11	A
12	D	12	D	12	D
13	E	13	B	13	A
14	B	14	C	14	B
15	D	15	B	15	A
16	A	16	B	16	A
17	C	17	D	17	A
18	C	18	E	18	D
19	B	19	D	19	E
20	E	20	A	20	E
21	E	21	C	21	A
22	A	22	B	22	D
23	B	23	B	23	D
24	D	24	B	24	A
25	C	25	D	25	D
26	D	26	C	26	A
27	D	27	A	27	D
28	C	28	E	28	D
29	E	29	D		
30	D	30	A		

Test 2 Answer Key

Section 1: Quantitative		Section 2: Verbal		Section 3: Reading	
Question	Answer	Question	Answer	Question	Answer
1	B	1	C	1	C
2	D	2	E	2	D
3	A	3	C	3	A
4	D	4	A	4	E
5	B	5	D	5	A
6	B	6	A	6	B
7	C	7	B	7	D
8	D	8	A	8	C
9	E	9	E	9	D
10	A	10	C	10	B
11	A	11	E	11	D
12	D	12	A	12	B
13	A	13	B	13	A
14	C	14	D	14	B
15	A	15	B	15	D
16	A	16	E	16	D
17	A	17	C	17	C
18	D	18	C	18	A
19	E	19	B	19	B
20	C	20	A	20	E
21	D	21	D	21	A
22	C	22	A	22	A
23	A	23	D	23	D
24	A	24	B	24	A
25	B	25	B	25	A
26	B	26	B	26	D
27	D	27	A	27	A
28	A	28	E	28	A
29	A	29	D		
30	D	30	A		

Test 3 Answer Key

Section 1: Quantitative		Section 2: Verbal		Section 3: Reading	
Question	Answer	Question	Answer	Question	Answer
1	D	1	C	1	D
2	E	2	B	2	C
3	A	3	B	3	A
4	B	4	A	4	D
5	A	5	A	5	B
6	D	6	D	6	E
7	A	7	C	7	E
8	E	8	D	8	A
9	E	9	C	9	C
10	D	10	E	10	A
11	D	11	B	11	E
12	C	12	E	12	E
13	E	13	A	13	E
14	C	14	D	14	C
15	B	15	B	15	E
16	B	16	C	16	C
17	B	17	D	17	A
18	B	18	D	18	D
19	A	19	D	19	C
20	C	20	B	20	A
21	B	21	C	21	B
22	B	22	B	22	A
23	C	23	D	23	E
24	E	24	C	24	A
25	A	25	D	25	C
26	C	26	D	26	E
27	D	27	C	27	D
28	E	28	C	28	C
29	B	29	E		
30	D	30	D		

CPSIA information can be obtained
at www.ICGtesting.com
Printed in the USA
BVHW051943280120
570744BV00014B/290